MILEAGE LOG

MAKE:		MODEL:		YEAR:
DATE:	**ODOMETER:** START | END		**TOTAL:**	**DESTINATION / PURPOSE:**

MILEAGE LOG

MAKE:		MODEL:		YEAR:
DATE:	**ODOMETER:** **START | END**		**TOTAL:**	**DESTINATION /** **PURPOSE:**

MILEAGE LOG

MAKE:	MODEL:	YEAR:	
DATE:	**ODOMETER:** **START | END**	**TOTAL:**	**DESTINATION /** **PURPOSE:**

MILEAGE LOG

MAKE:		MODEL:		YEAR:
DATE:	ODOMETER: START | END		TOTAL:	DESTINATION / PURPOSE:

MILEAGE LOG

MAKE:		MODEL:		YEAR:
DATE:	**ODOMETER:** **START | END**		**TOTAL:**	**DESTINATION /** **PURPOSE:**

MILEAGE LOG

MAKE:		MODEL:		YEAR:
DATE:	ODOMETER: START | END		TOTAL:	DESTINATION / PURPOSE:

MILEAGE LOG

MAKE:		MODEL:		YEAR:
DATE:	ODOMETER: START | END		TOTAL:	DESTINATION / PURPOSE:

MILEAGE LOG

MAKE:		MODEL:		YEAR:
DATE:	**ODOMETER:** **START | END**		**TOTAL:**	**DESTINATION / PURPOSE:**

MILEAGE LOG

MAKE:		MODEL:		YEAR:
DATE:	**ODOMETER:** **START | END**		**TOTAL:**	**DESTINATION / PURPOSE:**

MILEAGE LOG

MAKE:		MODEL:		YEAR:
DATE:	**ODOMETER:** **START | END**		**TOTAL:**	**DESTINATION /** **PURPOSE:**

MILEAGE LOG

MAKE:			MODEL:		YEAR:

DATE:	ODOMETER: START | END		TOTAL:	DESTINATION / PURPOSE:

MILEAGE LOG

MAKE:		MODEL:		YEAR:
DATE:	**ODOMETER:** **START | END**		**TOTAL:**	**DESTINATION / PURPOSE:**

MILEAGE LOG

MAKE:		MODEL:		YEAR:
DATE:	**ODOMETER:** **START | END**		**TOTAL:**	**DESTINATION /** **PURPOSE:**

MILEAGE LOG

MAKE:		MODEL:		YEAR:
DATE:	**ODOMETER:** **START | END**		**TOTAL:**	**DESTINATION /** **PURPOSE:**

MILEAGE LOG

MAKE:		MODEL:		YEAR:
DATE:	**ODOMETER:** **START | END**		**TOTAL:**	**DESTINATION /** **PURPOSE:**

MILEAGE LOG

MAKE:		MODEL:		YEAR:
DATE:	ODOMETER: START | END		TOTAL:	DESTINATION / PURPOSE:

MILEAGE LOG

MAKE:		MODEL:		YEAR:
DATE:	**ODOMETER:** **START | END**		**TOTAL:**	**DESTINATION /** **PURPOSE:**

MILEAGE LOG

MAKE:		MODEL:		YEAR:
DATE:	**ODOMETER:** **START | END**		**TOTAL:**	**DESTINATION / PURPOSE:**

MILEAGE LOG

MAKE:		MODEL:		YEAR:
DATE:	**ODOMETER:** **START | END**		**TOTAL:**	**DESTINATION / PURPOSE:**

MILEAGE LOG

MAKE:		MODEL:		YEAR:
DATE:	**ODOMETER:** **START | END**		**TOTAL:**	**DESTINATION /** **PURPOSE:**

MILEAGE LOG

MAKE:		MODEL:		YEAR:
DATE:	**ODOMETER:** **START | END**		**TOTAL:**	**DESTINATION / PURPOSE:**

MILEAGE LOG

MAKE:		MODEL:		YEAR:
DATE:	**ODOMETER:** START | END		**TOTAL:**	**DESTINATION / PURPOSE:**

MILEAGE LOG

MAKE:			MODEL:	YEAR:

DATE:	ODOMETER: START | END		TOTAL:	DESTINATION / PURPOSE:

MILEAGE LOG

MAKE:		MODEL:		YEAR:
DATE:	ODOMETER: START | END		TOTAL:	DESTINATION / PURPOSE:

MILEAGE LOG

MAKE:		MODEL:		YEAR:
DATE:	**ODOMETER:** **START | END**		**TOTAL:**	**DESTINATION /** **PURPOSE:**

MILEAGE LOG

MAKE:		MODEL:		YEAR:	
DATE:	**ODOMETER:** **START | END**		**TOTAL:**	**DESTINATION /** **PURPOSE:**	

MILEAGE LOG

MAKE:		MODEL:		YEAR:
DATE:	ODOMETER: START | END		TOTAL:	DESTINATION / PURPOSE:

MILEAGE LOG

MAKE:	MODEL:		YEAR:
DATE:	**ODOMETER:** **START | END**	**TOTAL:**	**DESTINATION /** **PURPOSE:**

MILEAGE LOG

MAKE:	MODEL:		YEAR:
DATE:	**ODOMETER:** **START | END**	**TOTAL:**	**DESTINATION /** **PURPOSE:**

MILEAGE LOG

MAKE:		MODEL:		YEAR:
DATE:	**ODOMETER:** **START | END**		**TOTAL:**	**DESTINATION /** **PURPOSE:**

MILEAGE LOG

MAKE:		MODEL:		YEAR:
DATE:	**ODOMETER:** **START | END**		**TOTAL:**	**DESTINATION /** **PURPOSE:**

MILEAGE LOG

MAKE:		MODEL:		YEAR:
DATE:	**ODOMETER:** **START | END**		**TOTAL:**	**DESTINATION /** **PURPOSE:**

MILEAGE LOG

MAKE:		MODEL:		YEAR:
DATE:	**ODOMETER:** **START | END**		**TOTAL:**	**DESTINATION /** **PURPOSE:**

MILEAGE LOG

MAKE:		MODEL:		YEAR:
DATE:	**ODOMETER:** **START | END**		**TOTAL:**	**DESTINATION /** **PURPOSE:**

MILEAGE LOG

MAKE:		MODEL:		YEAR:
DATE:	**ODOMETER:** START | END		**TOTAL:**	**DESTINATION / PURPOSE:**

MILEAGE LOG

MAKE:		MODEL:		YEAR:
DATE:	**ODOMETER:** **START | END**		**TOTAL:**	**DESTINATION /** **PURPOSE:**

MILEAGE LOG

MAKE:		MODEL:		YEAR:
DATE:	**ODOMETER:** **START | END**		**TOTAL:**	**DESTINATION /** **PURPOSE:**

MILEAGE LOG

MAKE:		MODEL:		YEAR:
DATE:	**ODOMETER:** **START | END**		**TOTAL:**	**DESTINATION /** **PURPOSE:**

MILEAGE LOG

MAKE:		MODEL:		YEAR:
DATE:	**ODOMETER:** **START | END**		**TOTAL:**	**DESTINATION / PURPOSE:**

MILEAGE LOG

MAKE:		MODEL:		YEAR:
DATE:	**ODOMETER:** **START | END**		**TOTAL:**	**DESTINATION /** **PURPOSE:**

MILEAGE LOG

MAKE:		MODEL:		YEAR:
DATE:	**ODOMETER:** **START | END**		**TOTAL:**	**DESTINATION / PURPOSE:**

MILEAGE LOG

MAKE:	MODEL:		YEAR:	
DATE:	ODOMETER: START | END		TOTAL:	DESTINATION / PURPOSE:

MILEAGE LOG

MAKE:		MODEL:		YEAR:
DATE:	ODOMETER: START | END		TOTAL:	DESTINATION / PURPOSE:

MILEAGE LOG

MAKE:		MODEL:		YEAR:
DATE:	**ODOMETER:** **START | END**		**TOTAL:**	**DESTINATION /** **PURPOSE:**

MILEAGE LOG

MAKE:	MODEL:		YEAR:	
DATE:	ODOMETER: START | END		TOTAL:	DESTINATION / PURPOSE:

MILEAGE LOG

MAKE:		MODEL:		YEAR:
DATE:	ODOMETER: START | END		TOTAL:	DESTINATION / PURPOSE:

MILEAGE LOG

MAKE:		MODEL:		YEAR:
DATE:	**ODOMETER:** **START | END**		**TOTAL:**	**DESTINATION / PURPOSE:**

MILEAGE LOG

MAKE:		MODEL:		YEAR:
DATE:	**ODOMETER: START | END**		**TOTAL:**	**DESTINATION / PURPOSE:**

MILEAGE LOG

MAKE:		MODEL:		YEAR:
DATE:	ODOMETER: START | END		TOTAL:	DESTINATION / PURPOSE:

MILEAGE LOG

MAKE:		MODEL:		YEAR:
DATE:	ODOMETER: START | END		TOTAL:	DESTINATION / PURPOSE:

MILEAGE LOG

MAKE:		MODEL:		YEAR:
DATE:	**ODOMETER:** **START | END**		**TOTAL:**	**DESTINATION / PURPOSE:**

MILEAGE LOG

MAKE:		MODEL:		YEAR:
DATE:	**ODOMETER:** **START | END**		**TOTAL:**	**DESTINATION /** **PURPOSE:**

MILEAGE LOG

MAKE:		MODEL:		YEAR:
DATE:	ODOMETER: START | END		TOTAL:	DESTINATION / PURPOSE:

MILEAGE LOG

MAKE:		MODEL:		YEAR:

DATE:	ODOMETER: START | END		TOTAL:	DESTINATION / PURPOSE:

MILEAGE LOG

MAKE:		MODEL:		YEAR:
DATE:	**ODOMETER:** **START | END**		**TOTAL:**	**DESTINATION /** **PURPOSE:**

MILEAGE LOG

MAKE:		MODEL:		YEAR:
DATE:	**ODOMETER:** **START | END**		**TOTAL:**	**DESTINATION /** **PURPOSE:**

MILEAGE LOG

MAKE:		MODEL:		YEAR:
DATE:	**ODOMETER:** **START | END**		**TOTAL:**	**DESTINATION / PURPOSE:**

MILEAGE LOG

MAKE:		MODEL:		YEAR:
DATE:	ODOMETER: START | END		TOTAL:	DESTINATION / PURPOSE:

MILEAGE LOG

MAKE:		MODEL:		YEAR:
DATE:	**ODOMETER:** **START | END**		**TOTAL:**	**DESTINATION /** **PURPOSE:**

MILEAGE LOG

MAKE:		MODEL:		YEAR:
DATE:	ODOMETER: START | END		TOTAL:	DESTINATION / PURPOSE:

MILEAGE LOG

MAKE:		MODEL:		YEAR:
DATE:	**ODOMETER:** **START | END**		**TOTAL:**	**DESTINATION /** **PURPOSE:**

MILEAGE LOG

MAKE:		MODEL:		YEAR:
DATE:	**ODOMETER: START | END**		**TOTAL:**	**DESTINATION / PURPOSE:**

MILEAGE LOG

MAKE:	MODEL:		YEAR:	
DATE:	**ODOMETER:** **START | END**		**TOTAL:**	**DESTINATION /** **PURPOSE:**

MILEAGE LOG

MAKE:		MODEL:		YEAR:
DATE:	**ODOMETER:** **START | END**		**TOTAL:**	**DESTINATION / PURPOSE:**

MILEAGE LOG

MAKE:		MODEL:		YEAR:
DATE:	**ODOMETER:** **START | END**		**TOTAL:**	**DESTINATION /** **PURPOSE:**

MILEAGE LOG

MAKE:		MODEL:		YEAR:
DATE:	ODOMETER: START | END		TOTAL:	DESTINATION / PURPOSE:

MILEAGE LOG

MAKE:		MODEL:		YEAR:
DATE:	**ODOMETER:** **START | END**		**TOTAL:**	**DESTINATION /** **PURPOSE:**

MILEAGE LOG

MAKE:		MODEL:		YEAR:
DATE:	ODOMETER: START | END		TOTAL:	DESTINATION / PURPOSE:

MILEAGE LOG

MAKE:		MODEL:		YEAR:
DATE:	ODOMETER: START | END		TOTAL:	DESTINATION / PURPOSE:

MILEAGE LOG

MAKE:		MODEL:		YEAR:	
DATE:	**ODOMETER:** **START | END**		**TOTAL:**	**DESTINATION /** **PURPOSE:**	

MILEAGE LOG

MAKE:		MODEL:		YEAR:	
DATE:	ODOMETER: START | END		TOTAL:	DESTINATION / PURPOSE:	

MILEAGE LOG

MAKE:		MODEL:		YEAR:
DATE:	ODOMETER: START | END		TOTAL:	DESTINATION / PURPOSE:

MILEAGE LOG

MAKE:		MODEL:		YEAR:
DATE:	**ODOMETER:** **START | END**		**TOTAL:**	**DESTINATION /** **PURPOSE:**

MILEAGE LOG

MAKE:		MODEL:		YEAR:
DATE:	ODOMETER: START | END		TOTAL:	DESTINATION / PURPOSE:

MILEAGE LOG

MAKE:		MODEL:		YEAR:
DATE:	**ODOMETER:** **START | END**		**TOTAL:**	**DESTINATION / PURPOSE:**

MILEAGE LOG

DATE:	ODOMETER: START | END		TOTAL:	DESTINATION / PURPOSE:
MAKE:		MODEL:		YEAR:

MILEAGE LOG

MAKE:		MODEL:		YEAR:
DATE:	ODOMETER: START | END		TOTAL:	DESTINATION / PURPOSE:

MILEAGE LOG

MAKE:		MODEL:		YEAR:
DATE:	**ODOMETER:** **START | END**		**TOTAL:**	**DESTINATION /** **PURPOSE:**

MILEAGE LOG

MAKE:		MODEL:		YEAR:
DATE:	**ODOMETER:** **START | END**		**TOTAL:**	**DESTINATION / PURPOSE:**

MILEAGE LOG

MAKE:		MODEL:		YEAR:
DATE:	ODOMETER: START | END		TOTAL:	DESTINATION / PURPOSE:

MILEAGE LOG

MAKE:		MODEL:		YEAR:
DATE:	ODOMETER: START | END		TOTAL:	DESTINATION / PURPOSE:

MILEAGE LOG

MAKE:		MODEL:		YEAR:
DATE:	**ODOMETER:** **START | END**		**TOTAL:**	**DESTINATION /** **PURPOSE:**

MILEAGE LOG

MAKE:		MODEL:		YEAR:	
DATE:		ODOMETER: START | END		TOTAL:	DESTINATION / PURPOSE:

MILEAGE LOG

MAKE:		MODEL:		YEAR:
DATE:	**ODOMETER:** **START | END**		**TOTAL:**	**DESTINATION / PURPOSE:**

MILEAGE LOG

MAKE:		MODEL:		YEAR:
DATE:	**ODOMETER:** **START | END**		**TOTAL:**	**DESTINATION /** **PURPOSE:**

MILEAGE LOG

MAKE:		MODEL:		YEAR:
DATE:	**ODOMETER:** **START | END**		**TOTAL:**	**DESTINATION / PURPOSE:**

MILEAGE LOG

DATE:	ODOMETER: START | END		TOTAL:	DESTINATION / PURPOSE:

MAKE: **MODEL:**   **YEAR:**

DATE:	ODOMETER: START | END		TOTAL:	DESTINATION / PURPOSE:

MILEAGE LOG

MAKE:		MODEL:		YEAR:
DATE:	**ODOMETER:** **START | END**		**TOTAL:**	**DESTINATION /** **PURPOSE:**

MILEAGE LOG

MAKE:		MODEL:		YEAR:
DATE:	ODOMETER: START | END		TOTAL:	DESTINATION / PURPOSE:

MILEAGE LOG

MAKE:		MODEL:		YEAR:
DATE:	ODOMETER: START | END		TOTAL:	DESTINATION / PURPOSE:

MILEAGE LOG

MAKE:		MODEL:		YEAR:
DATE:	ODOMETER: START | END		TOTAL:	DESTINATION / PURPOSE:

MILEAGE LOG

MAKE:		MODEL:		YEAR:
DATE:	**ODOMETER:** **START | END**		**TOTAL:**	**DESTINATION /** **PURPOSE:**

MILEAGE LOG

MAKE:		MODEL:		YEAR:
DATE:	**ODOMETER:** **START | END**		**TOTAL:**	**DESTINATION / PURPOSE:**

MILEAGE LOG

MAKE:		MODEL:		YEAR:
DATE:	ODOMETER: START | END		TOTAL:	DESTINATION / PURPOSE:

MILEAGE LOG

MAKE:		MODEL:		YEAR:
DATE:	ODOMETER: START | END		TOTAL:	DESTINATION / PURPOSE:

MILEAGE LOG

MAKE:		MODEL:		YEAR:
DATE:	ODOMETER: START | END		TOTAL:	DESTINATION / PURPOSE:

MILEAGE LOG

MAKE:		MODEL:		YEAR:
DATE:	**ODOMETER:** **START | END**		**TOTAL:**	**DESTINATION / PURPOSE:**

MILEAGE LOG

MAKE:		MODEL:		YEAR:
DATE:	ODOMETER: START | END		TOTAL:	DESTINATION / PURPOSE:

MILEAGE LOG

MAKE:		MODEL:		YEAR:
DATE:	**ODOMETER:** **START | END**		**TOTAL:**	**DESTINATION / PURPOSE:**

MILEAGE LOG

MAKE:		MODEL:		YEAR:
DATE:	**ODOMETER:** **START | END**		**TOTAL:**	**DESTINATION /** **PURPOSE:**

MILEAGE LOG

MAKE:		MODEL:		YEAR:
DATE:	ODOMETER: START | END		TOTAL:	DESTINATION / PURPOSE:

MILEAGE LOG

MAKE:		MODEL:		YEAR:
DATE:	ODOMETER: START | END		TOTAL:	DESTINATION / PURPOSE:

MILEAGE LOG

MAKE:		MODEL:		YEAR:
DATE:	**ODOMETER:** **START | END**		**TOTAL:**	**DESTINATION /** **PURPOSE:**

MILEAGE LOG

MAKE:		MODEL:		YEAR:
DATE:	ODOMETER: START | END		TOTAL:	DESTINATION / PURPOSE:

MILEAGE LOG

MAKE:		MODEL:		YEAR:
DATE:	**ODOMETER:** **START | END**		**TOTAL:**	**DESTINATION /** **PURPOSE:**

MILEAGE LOG

MAKE:		MODEL:		YEAR:	
DATE:	**ODOMETER:** **START | END**		**TOTAL:**	**DESTINATION / PURPOSE:**	

MILEAGE LOG

MAKE:		MODEL:		YEAR:
DATE:	**ODOMETER:** **START | END**		**TOTAL:**	**DESTINATION /** **PURPOSE:**

MILEAGE LOG

MAKE:		MODEL:		YEAR:
DATE:	ODOMETER: START | END		TOTAL:	DESTINATION / PURPOSE:

MILEAGE LOG

MAKE:		MODEL:		YEAR:
DATE:	ODOMETER: START | END		TOTAL:	DESTINATION / PURPOSE:

MILEAGE LOG

MAKE:		MODEL:		YEAR:	
DATE:	**ODOMETER:** **START | END**		**TOTAL:**	**DESTINATION /** **PURPOSE:**	

MILEAGE LOG

MAKE:		MODEL:		YEAR:
DATE:	**ODOMETER:** **START | END**		**TOTAL:**	**DESTINATION /** **PURPOSE:**

MILEAGE LOG

MAKE:		MODEL:		YEAR:
DATE:	**ODOMETER:** **START | END**		**TOTAL:**	**DESTINATION / PURPOSE:**

MILEAGE LOG

MAKE:		MODEL:		YEAR:
DATE:	ODOMETER: START | END		TOTAL:	DESTINATION / PURPOSE:

MILEAGE LOG

MAKE:		MODEL:		YEAR:
DATE:	ODOMETER: START | END		TOTAL:	DESTINATION / PURPOSE:

MILEAGE LOG

MAKE:		MODEL:		YEAR:
DATE:	ODOMETER: START | END		TOTAL:	DESTINATION / PURPOSE:

MILEAGE LOG

MAKE:		MODEL:		YEAR:
DATE:	**ODOMETER:** **START | END**		**TOTAL:**	**DESTINATION /** **PURPOSE:**

MILEAGE LOG

MAKE:		MODEL:		YEAR:
DATE:	**ODOMETER:** **START | END**		**TOTAL:**	**DESTINATION /** **PURPOSE:**

MILEAGE LOG

MAKE:		MODEL:		YEAR:
DATE:	ODOMETER: START | END		TOTAL:	DESTINATION / PURPOSE:

MILEAGE LOG

MAKE:		MODEL:		YEAR:
DATE:	**ODOMETER:** **START | END**		**TOTAL:**	**DESTINATION /** **PURPOSE:**

MILEAGE LOG

MAKE:		MODEL:		YEAR:
DATE:	**ODOMETER:** **START | END**		**TOTAL:**	**DESTINATION /** **PURPOSE:**

Made in the USA
Middletown, DE
03 March 2023

26143794R00071